Monarchs Fly Great Distances

Monarchs Fly Great Distances

Poems by

Barbara Wuest

Kelsay Books

Cover Design by Linda Watts
Cover Photograph by Anthony Marino

ISBN: 13- 978-1-947465-47-3

Kelsay Books
Aldrich Press
www.kelsaybooks.com

For my mother
Vivian McInturff Ripley
(1922-1996)

Contents

Monarchs Fly Great Distances

a.

Lines at the edge of a monarch's wing
travel to the body where the weight is.

I imagine our minds arranged this way.
Chaos and lace. Signals received
in the middle, in the nick
of time, I am never where the call comes in.

Where oh where,
question from the child
choosing
designs that turn up
unfamiliar,
to be chased,
but for now…

Shock. We are tall and cease
looking down.

Eyes straight ahead or skybound,
keen for the cosmos and our own
dead aim toward future selves,
we're adult and the stocks are down.

But not on literal ground, sorry to say,
worm-life lost on the best of us.

b.

As I watched it crawl across my palm
I didn't know
it had been one
of 400 eggs
laid
on a milkweed leaf.

I didn't know its shell had changed from yellow to gray,
I didn't know it had taken two weeks to become this soft,
I didn't know
furry things move, and slowly enough
for us
to study, on their own terms,
their wool gathering wet wings dying to dry,
and light.

c.

Without them I wouldn't have been a child, or know.
Nor you.

"If you do not raise your eyes
you will think that you
are the highest point," the Italian Argentine wrote.
Did he say it first? I wonder.

d.

Wires crossed: I imagine, I think, I feel
the sheets and the ink will be dry
before the rain begins.

Not to mention
my gut tells me, and *God* as well,
on the horizon, going with the flow.

Even though, *ex nihilo*, on every last wing
orange shows up to warn the others there
may be danger in color so ridiculously bright.

Dear Predators: You might see red in the yellow.
One angry enough to kill is a coward
say the histories
of the shades
we name.
Yours,

e.

But there I was at the San Juan Capistrano Mission.
There I was, delighting in coincidence:
writing about monarchs on the same day
one shows up in front of us, flitting over the roses.

It
had nothing to say. It
had no interest in meaning
anything to me.
All it "said" was: that it was, no more,
no less, as it flew over the ruined wall
exposed to the sun like us.

f.

You return to a place to explain your love.
Or reclaim your right to exist alongside its persistent
tic you sense in your skin, your voice,
your heart, in your skull, your brain
or somewhere.

g.

I have been sad there, in the sacred garden,
looking up at the original bells
and reproductions gotten so right
the docent needs to show which is which.

I have been glad when the stones underfoot
bring the workers to mind, workers
who rise
more than eye-level when I stand
real still.

h.

Every so often the brochure is revised.

Bougainvillea blooms near an arch that survived.

How many cameras have taken this scene
stuck in a file for the heirs to find
and think not of the flowers but the hand in time,
not of the doorway but the hand
in time.

i.

A plaque embedded in the brick says
the Nixons rang the bell cast in iron
in 1904
on March 22, 1969.

And marked by its bright green signs,
its never-ending lines,
the 5 drones on
past the big thick walls surrounding our tour, car after car
coming for to carry
our going

j.

where we need to light
or locale's no more
than a windshield away,

hood, light, front bumper,
road

keep a safe distance

from the numbers in front
embossed on plates
from many other states.

k.

Place is a street.
Place is a square, a circle, a diamond
where the bases are: first, second, third, home—

where oh where

"I feel like I want to go home
and I don't know where home is."

My mother said it and I wrote it down
here where home is,
where I am at home in the stops and starts
punctuation demands, and in
the spaces between.

l.

Out of nothing, we are richly out of nothing.

Born not made we make our way, you do, I do.
It is time to grow young, it is time to return.

Bent over like an apostrophe,
hanging on like a comma, the dying I thrives.

m.

Large migrating butterflies can't know
the rubber-to-the-road danger
and freedom a large mammal
learns from the seat of a Toyota or a Ford.

When drivers "fly" they are going too fast.
There are smash-ups.

A monarch flies into the path of the wrong bird.
Or a child catches it, finally, in a jar.
She pokes holes in the lid and still it dies.

n o

where is its soul, where's yours, where's mine

p.

A power much lower answers:
There was a child who occupied
the grown woman for years, made
of her body a small country where
citizens lived in peace until one day
she let out a cry their ears could barely
receive, a cry too ready not to stay long.

q.r.s.t.u.v.w.x.y.z.

In the domiciles and homes
on the streets of our towns
in the land that we love,
the only laws we obey
are the letters of the laws
in the letter of the law,
the letter of the law
we break or deny or ignore
in the name of the imprisoned
in the name of the free.

a.

Din finally done we-the-people now rest, assured our
souls (all alone) neither light where we are, nor light.

b.

So we hold ourselves up by holding
ourselves down, describing to a tee
the way a frond waves back, as we
sit on our hands, giddy in the sand.

c.

The science lab had a putrid smell.
She walked in timidly and sat down
on a stool near a long black table.

Across from her on the green wall
she saw them lined up, one of each
species pinned to a field of cotton.

Cellophane covered their bodies
and wings, a cardboard frame
held the many designs in place.

She could not sit still on the stool.
Her socks, which she'd washed in
the sink the night before, were wet.

She finally had the cramps others
had been having for a year or two.
The teacher led them to a page

in their books and said the word
slowly, *tax-on-o-my,* the accent
on the second syllable, he said.

Seeing the word then watching
his lips she whispered *taxonomy*
and her cramps eased up just a bit.

You not only have to know how
to pronounce it, you also have to
know how to define taxonomy.

His jaw moved up and down.
She imagined him kissing his
wife, she blushed, she shivered.

Two Ways

A. The Cemetery Way

In an age when the holy's not holy
anymore we have, for that matter, still,

these signs in the rough
stone of the distant past,
the polished of recent years.

***

The Woman and the Fawn: A Story

At the end of her walk among the many tombs
she spies in the tall grass a doe and her fawn.
Odd how they make your back straighten up,
she thinks, gawking at the wonder they are
moving in the green, beautifully themselves.

We are at ease on the earth then all of it shifts:
the fawn loses track of the doe—makes a gap—
leaps to the path that the people use, follows
the woman who's mistaken for the mama doe.
The woman's aware there is something amiss,

the woman knows the fawn is confused. Yet,
she keeps on going, alert to the life-giving fear
their shadows bring to the very strange scene
they are starring in, the woman and the fawn,
the dead all around, and the dead, all around.

She stops, turns, startles the fawn who tries to
step back, falls, all four legs sticking out like
twigs, its eyes meeting hers in eternal pause
the two of them sensing there is something
brand new under this June sun's high noon.

The fawn gets up, follows her again down the
people's road, the woman who knows there is
something she should do to make things right
when the fawn darts farther from the doe who
entreats the woman who fails at the close…

***

We want babies and we get them.
We want more babies and we get them.

And then one day,
we get a baby
we don't get
to keep.

It only takes one
to make the world mourn,
to sting our hearts, to stop us
short at the stores and squeeze
our young who have made their ways

and stayed.

It only takes one for sleep not to come.
It only takes one for the night to go wrong.

***

Scared by the letters running down the post
I
N
F
A
N
T
S
I paced back and forth, there was something
I should do because there they were—

all the *ones*
laid beneath offerings
none of them can touch:

pinwheels and bears and angels so heavy
they can't leave the ground that slopes
west to east
and fades into woods
full of living
deer.

***

Should there be a root
more courtly than God it would be
a reading of the names
one   by   one
one   by   inimitable   one
one

***

What have I to do with a face gone to seed?
I ask as I wander through the somber streets.

Mostly there are names and the crucial years.
Only an occasional "gone home" appears.

Choosing good words to sum up our lives
belongs, it seems, to more certain times.

Except for the one
at the northern edge, the one named Kress
who bothered to say as I passed all alone:
"I hope you dance like no one is watching."

"Well, yes, Mr. Kress. I guess I've the time,
since you bothered to say, I mean write, to me."

I removed my shoes and threw them in the woods,
unpinned my hair and let it fall all over my face,
placed my finger, the pointer, on top of my head,
twirled in time to the epitaph, twirled so long I fell
to the ground and slept, at last, at last like the dead!

***

And a breeze still arrives in mercy's guise.
I'm allowed to go on and the hills still roll.

There's a Holy Ghost Drive and a Trinity
Road in this "city" they call Mount Calvary
where I'm blessed to be on a day too nice
for anyone to stroll on a cemetery's knolls.

As a digger unearths more places for the dead
my own deep rest shakes another place loose:

I remember a spot under L.A.'s sun
in a pretty courtyard on Kingsley Drive:
At the center of the entrance stands one tree
whose trunk reaches to the second floor,
whose branches lean on each end roof
like the elbows of a gatekeeper.

I face this tree from the window of a corner flat.
Morning, the tenants are gone to work or still
asleep as I watch the sun push its way in, stuffing
the gray remnants of night behind the bushes.

Amid all this green, one pink flower bows
from a clematis vine like a hatted worshiper.

I see myself there, shaded under a brim some
Easter Sunday in the past or the future, falling
or perhaps limping home in a believer's dress.

But it's still January and I notice that a jade
near the window sprouts white blossoms as
pure as snowflakes or tiny stars, and beyond,
a rectangular patch of leaves grows close
to the ground, hands raised in a cluster, palms
turned up, receiving the sun in gold coins.

Near the leaves stands a table, round like those
along turquoise pools where drinks are served
with fruit biting into the sides of curved glass.

I open the window, press a jade leaf between
thumb and finger, a thin red line follows its
contour, I can almost feel a pulse, I want to
slip inside, bathe in the juice it holds, sit
in its first pew with soil under my feet
and nothing but roots on the altar.

***

What is the underground
portion or descending
axis of a plant, which
absorbs moisture,
obtains or stores
nourishment,
and provides
support?
Young shirtless workers mow around
the grounds of the young they survive.
It is hot and they sweat and they mow
and I can't stop circling these avenues.

A shrine behind glass leads to the yard
where the babies carry the inadequate
symbols parents-in-ruin sadly provide.
I look in at the statue that was crowned
in Prague and dressed in a vestment fit
only for an earthbound queen or a king.

I cannot tell the sex of the lost fawn
anymore than I can tell the sex of this
royal child whose right hand blesses our

very being, the first two fingers raised,
one for the human and one for divine,
the lowered thumb and the other two

holding the mystery of famous threes:
the mother and the father and the child,
creators and redeemers and sanctifiers.

So much contained in the statue's right
hand it's hard to study its time-honored
left, the world balanced in its tiny palm.

The list of miracles is written in a book:
Water is restored to a town and a brain-
damaged boy reasons again…thanks

to the infant with the whole world in its
hand, the earth and the sky, in its hand,
you and me, in its hand, everybody here…

***

…the wind and the rain, in its hand, you
and me, in its hand, the earth and the sky…

Lana had everything, a house by the shore
and a loft in the city where friends brought
recipes from Rome, stirred glorious pastas
on days when the weather forced them in.

And she told them life is abrupt and full.
"So sudden," she added, looking into
puzzled and rosy-rich faces entreatingly.
I tell you I can't go back and I can't go on

yet it's all I've ever known, these two ways,
all I've ever had to know, seventy odd years
removed from some root nobody's made
a good likeness of, no one's come close,

though Hopper's *High Noon* may,
with its woman in the long blue robe
standing at the door of her white frame
house as if waiting for a lover who will

always be arriving or not, arriving or not.
I was gone in my need to say it all, so far
gone the guests went to bed and there I was
in my house by the shore smelling old garlic,

testing the echo when, suddenly, Lana said:
No place works long enough for the orphans
roaming the streets, no location has what it
takes, and I asked what in God's name she

was talking about and she lowered her voice,
saying how ridiculous it was to stand on my
soapbox, losing, as if my family hadn't taught
me the dangers of going full throttle this way.

Once the birth-givers pass their torch, they turn
us loose and the *I* never knows where it's speaking
from, when a scraped knee burns, or kisses feel like
the very end, or the eyes of the guests close too soon.

***

The time just ahead coupling
with that just behind, copulating,
trying to bear fruit, as if eternity

could ever be a tree

shaken by the next location, or killed,
hauled off on a flatbed truck, the losing
waving to their lost, their lost once again.

We say this to ourselves, I do,

knowing no better than the tree.

***

The large scary space of my memory
moved toward things,
a doll to hold:
blue marble eyes,
roselike cheeks,
mouth open to receive
the small bottle of water
I promised to give,
if only I'd find her on Christmas Day,
Tiny Tears, name I saw
in a book, the source of desire.

I wanted things, and to be other than I was:
in a dream I was riding on a blue bicycle,
balancing four children on the handlebars;
in another dream, shelves with four books.

***

Desire layered on our lives in the choir loft,
we sang the words on the music sheet, mouths
formed like the baby doll's, we'd practice
no na no, no na no, no na no
for the Latin we would sing
for the host.

***

I am the woman who failed at closing
the gap between the doe and her fawn.
This, and everything I say, is recalled:
the dream of practicing for Latin songs,
of balancing children and spying books.

After the fact, I open a book that smells
of age and disuse, its gold-lettered name
so eroded with time it is hard to read
down its withering, dirty-blue spine.

You are forced to open to the title page:

The Great and Little One of Prague
(a book about the infant in the glass-
enclosed shrine hosting all the ones
I listened for on the cemetery way)

by Ludvik Nemec

whose Nihil Obstat or "nothing stands in the way"
allowed for the Imprimatur that "let it be printed"
for all of us to read of the birth of the statue

(that stands for "the eternal Infancy of God")

in the midst of "the unhappy history of Prague."

The Thirty Years' War so "embittered the waters
of unrest" for the Czechs that the need was great
for seeing a sign in wood and wax, solid promise:
a little child to heal them, and lead them, to peace.

Looking in at the replica of the Infant of Prague
I saw none of the pain that the writer describes,
nor the needs of a people three centuries ago—
but I did see a statue of a child, lost in a gilded
robe, holding onto the world, as if it were light.

***

There are pinwheels too on the graves of adults—

silver and blue spinning in the sun
and I stop to rest on an old stone bench made
for the mourner who lingers in the open space
between loss and the thought that tries to fill in.

Around a large old stone lies a circle of priests
who died in the service of a church gone astray,
who died in the service of a people they loved.

This close to their bones I can hear their sighs.
The language they speak is one I was taught in
the days when order hadn't gotten out of hand.

I am in a dark wooden box hearing a male voice
telling me to sin no more and to say more words.

My dear priests, listen first to one of my dreams:
I was talking someone out of killing herself and
being offered the host on a piece of typing paper.

In my ignorance, I ate both, when everyone else,
knowing better than I, ate only the blessed host.

I sat in the corner—Jack turning over stones—
like and *as*, not forgetting *as good as* or just *is*.

I am sure you understand my dilemma: if all in
the world is good, if it's a good world after all,
and a small one, why is there good and better?

What is "hail holy queen mother of mercy" but
a royal call that muffles the sound of kneeling
on straw with no crown or dazzling blue robe?

See? We remember otherwise and our own
mothers, a pine tree inside and under it, gifts.

The confessional sits unused, its secrets exposed.
Dear priests, may you dream, may you freely
dream down to the root of our necessary lives.

***

(The noise outside is deafening as I try to recollect the Cemetery
Way, pave its streets for your consideration, line its grounds with
sorrowful songs and momentary joyful tunes, the way lives go,
tragedy constant somewhere in the world yet seized now and then
by the lightly. Noise outside is more deafening now. Another kind
of Angel has come to my town to oppose the ones made of stone,
the ones unable to leave the earth, and those standing guard over
every child's trusting shoulder.)

Dark blue planes swirl and twist against a light blue sky.

With our feet on the ground among thousands
we follow their wings as they weave around
buildings and over the Lake in deepest blue.
Feet on the ground and eyes in the air where
there is no limit to the forms they can take.
They zoom straight up and they disappear.

F/A-18 Hornets (Blue Angels)
the first dual-role fighter/attack aircraft
serving on the nation's front lines of defense.
The noise is deafening but the patterns satisfy
the curious eye, every last person looking up,
dark blue planes with lines of white smoke
swirl against a light blue sky in July.

* * * * * *

Desire layered on our pillows where
heads full of time pause for dramas
to unfold, invasions so crazy they're
forgotten for years, stuck. Dead weight.

Desire as much rock as cave. *Tantum*
ergo sacramentum, the Latin calls me
to see and hear and take it in, to come
adore this wondrous presence, want—
to want and to want and to want again.

I am Lana too but you already knew.

When there was nothing more to say,
I trusted in the new and the babies too.

My body begins once again to blend
with the space all around and what this
does is place the mind in a harrowing
stillness, the moments circulating
slowly   and you   looking at it all:
time   location   you
burgeoning in among the elements
as if you are here for the first time,
taking in sights and smells, touring
your own home
with a will to change every single room.

It's changes you once made that trip you up,
their logic eluding clear reason, but you won't be
embarrassed, you won't want to hide your mistakes.

You'll just wait, let time and grace do what they do,
and that too will bring you back where you've been,
and ahead where you'll be, sinking you, here and now,
until you think you are dead but your eyes simply widen
to see yourself dying, not denying the living you, finally.

***

No more weary than the earth
its trees risen to make the skyline sane,

no more weary
than the genes of the nomad
plucking her cello at Carnegie Hall,
this clamor within, the cries from below:

a morning alone, woods-and-deer
kind of place, retreatants draw near,
their histories so visibly dirt-rich
on their brows

I am changing again.

Sizzle of insects bores into my brain,
wakes a filament that never let go
of a tree-filled past: locust and oak,
cedar and maple and catalpa sprawl.

There's a cluster of cattails on the upper road.

My mind stumbles upon apples sliced
on a glass tray, a candle a few inches
high, the wick engaged with the flame,
the wicked engaged with the flame,
the wicked me engaged with the flame:

the only light on the array of apples
browning by the minute, rotting,
even out here, where divine's so
thick you can cut it with a knife,
where, quiet for days, talking arrives
carrying our risings on an earthen tray
that serves to our voices

a strange present tense.

B. The Tall Grass Way

At Ease on the Earth

Since weather speaks for itself, since pictures,
snapped by the people, freeze so many of its
moments that wouldn't have stayed otherwise,
weigh how we act in the face of its disregard.
It tears at our shores, topples our stores as we
run toward its fury, away, then back and away.
How alluring the rhythms of ferocious winds!
Yet seasons get old before their endings come.
Children are bored with the snow, their elders
fed up with the spring's late chill. We're tired.
Pulled low when it's nice, lifted when it's not,
we are seldom in touch with its roiling source.
Still, morning arrives and we raise the shade
saying once more, this time, maybe this time.

For the Night

Late fall, an orphan walks without shoes
in her grandmother's picked-over orchard.
She carries a basket anyway, heart filled
to the brim with fear, hatred, and shame.
A self-centered uncle had exposed himself,
touched her there, touched what was hers.
She fills her basket with the fallen fruit,
her shoulders stooped under empty limbs.
Twisted roots protrude from the ground.
Though she looks very old she floats as
a child, her feet touching nothing but air.
Oh Night, you lend her a path of all good:
Arranging it so that her father's not dead,
you deliver her body into arms she trusts.

Last Words

Now that I have your interest I never had in life
I will say what I know in stone under glaring sun:
Remember not to stop at the root of the problem.
Make hay with your singular brilliance posthaste.
Plan nothing, plan everything, plan nothing again.
Drink tea with your parents on Tuesday at three.
Search for enchantment in the absence of love.
Fall to your knees when your lies are exposed.
Hide among the Tall Grass and record its words.
Parse this list after dark by the light of the stars.
Honor the ability of your feet to feel the earth's
work, terrible and soft, even with your shoes on.
Ignore any sign gouged in granite that denies
you the tools for dredging up the new forthwith.

Jade Leaf

It's all the same to me,
she says all the time.

All the same? I ask defiantly. Can't be
the same, nothing is ever that way, the same.

She is jaded, you see, and all I can do is keep
showing her the buds on my plant, buds alongside

the leather-skinned leaves hanging over the
sides of the flower pot made for the lives of the jade.

The Underground Portion

It's the portion easy to ignore, better to look up
at the sleek blue planes flying in perfect formation,
watch astronauts flailing in space on our screens.
As we dream new life out there let us dwell with
the lives down below, children who've been seen
by the naked eye, bright as light in a July 4th sky.
Imagine the swift miracle of their months in flesh.
Before they had time to be tired of a toy or to long
for more than the day they were in, they were gone.
We wait for the lessons they are sure to give once
the noise of our prayers to the one on high recedes.
Only then will we hear their soft walks on the earth
unveiling the ways to accept all the joys that crest
and the genius in repeating *let us love* till we do.

House by the Shore

It exists in her head so vividly she hears
the waves and gulls in her deepest sleep.
Three at time would gather (Ms. Scotus
and two guests who would stay a week)
leave quietly before the sun comes up,
make way for the next two, the next…
Tea is served in bone china cups, scones
on plates to match, the drawing room so
civilized buried pain spirals out of control,
each one different from the last: Jan curses,
Ben laughs madly, Sarah sobs, Lana shakes,
Bill's hands tremble, Jim's struck dumb—
the hostess assembles all the signs, offers
one rare case at a time to the everywhere.

Things

Forgive us our living into the evening with
friends and bread, the deep stews of winter.
We are born with nothing to hold but thin air.
So we grab mama's finger, grip with our fist
which never stops searching for substitutes:
not just a cup but a pretty cup, not just a toy
but a melodic toy, not just a bear but a woolly
bear, not just a pinwheel but one I can see my-
self in, not just a doorknob but one I can turn.
I go in. There is a desk and a chair. I climb up,
leaf through the book lying open there. I see
a house, snow, footprints. I smell onions, go in.
Steam rises out of bowls that have pale yellow
roses painted on their sides. There are spoons.

Statue

An old Spanish monk received a vision from
the Child and carved its likeness in gratitude.
They say it passed into the hands of Theresa
of Avila who gave it as a wedding gift to a
Bohemian nobleman and his Spanish bride
who passed it on to their daughter Polyxema
who passed it on to barefooted Carmelites
in Prague which was soon invaded causing
the statue to be lost in the ruins until a priest
mended its hands, returned it to the oratory.
Miracles occurred, word spread, people came.
Three hundred years later pilgrims still travel
to pray to the statue that looks like an infant
but is dressed like a priest ready to say mass.

To Say More Words

is a way to grieve for
ourselves and the

woman who kneels
on straw beside
the child who's

alive in its
crib and dies
in her arms

as a grown-up
child, she mourns,
and the sculptor

chiseled their forms
for the times

Patterns

I walked each day in sunny June two ways:
a Cemetery Way, a Tall Grass way in wind.
I strolled alone as prairie growth sashayed
across my view and back and then within.
My eyes were closed and yet I saw the sky,
its streaks of white lit up my dullest bones.
The perfect blue that swept the outward rise
transformed my heart and lungs in even tones.
The sun came in and bathed my mind in light.
Then I could see the Cemetery Way as clear
as time and space and meaning all aligned,
good trio singing harmonies much freer.
The inside-out the outside-in recharged
so now I see the landscapes full and large.

This Wondrous Presence

Best, no doubt, not to call it nothing or something,
this touchable abstraction anyone knows and feels.
But before you know it the anyone who feels and
knows discovers the facts of his or her special case.
Not only the facts but also the act, anyone is caught
in the act then and catches herself believing in jade
and a wooden crib with a word one might choose.
There's a fawn, there's a baby, a patch of leaves.
Vine, worshiper, and hands raised in a cluster so
Lana chooses that word which is beyond all other
words she might consider as she talks two ways.
She believes in the holy that stands by her desk
asking her to hush without saying *stop saying*
replica and statue and dark blue planes, grace.

Dyings

Having come a long way and no way
I understand more and less than before.
The more carries voices of children,
the less contains questions that stay.
Young and old and in-between die
leaving readable traces we must not
ignore since they change with our
breathing commingling with why.
There is something to understand
that's as formless as time and as
wide as the space we build rooms
to contain all our best laid plans
becoming that way only because
we conspire with the fires of loss.

"engaged with the flame"

if in the past I have instead stayed back
or allowed myself to be consumed then
no more there is no turning around now
it remains right next to my desk with its
pen-dropping force its face only felt and
not seen and I am aware of its crowd-like
buzz and the pressures on the ear to make
its tones much less familiar so very much
since the voices of the dying and the dead
never sound the same no matter how many
rooms I build twelve or thirteen it matters
so little that I hear the child giggle to think
I would try to even things out in the end

Areas of Reverence

Area A:

Sex would restore us, then it wouldn't, then it

would again, the same with talk, so what we do next, what we

will into place this evening, is as chancy as our having been

brought together at all, with first talk,

then a note, and then sex, having no idea which it was

creating this present,

and presence, our pictures have yet to explain.

Not even the one of you in your suit and me in my

real silk dress, aqua as an artificial sea, walking by

a worn-out fence our hosts had strung with streamers

and balloons, announcing our place at the mariachi mass we would

soon take in, and forget, until now, when we say

we recall how right it had seemed to be tapping our feet

to songs that bring back the death, and its necessary life.

Area B:

I don't resist the temptation to lean down

into the crib, put my ear just above the baby's lips.

For that stolen moment I am offering him

all the world's cares, in exchange for a purifying love only

he can enflesh, love I can copy when

I walk toward the people I owe my listening to.

It's a frightening path, a frightening hour.

Forbid my leaving by the side door this

fear-of-your-difference lures me to, knowing what's next:

crush those words I was fortified to say.

Walking on tiles, heels of my shoes making

clacking sounds, I stop, close enough to hear

breathing so faint as not to be there but it is.

Area C:

In a narrow college classroom, I was introduced to

philosophy by a white-haired, skinny man who asked

if we had ever noticed that, at parties, everyone walks around

looking for the party, a question I remember after

one we had on a winter afternoon in Milwaukee.

We sat by the fireplace awhile, got up, moved to the

kitchen, ate stuffed mushrooms, sharp cheese,

tried to get the conversation going, asked a bored

teenager about the picture on his shirt saying *summit plummet.*

Searching for the party we learned about snowboards.

Soon there was a Bernese Mountain puppy in the arms

of a grown man and the guests kept stroking its paws.

Area D:

Muddy Waters' Face

If your hands were cold you could warm them there,

that's how fiery his cheeks, his lips, his eyes both

closed and feeling his song in the deep-down sweetness

of the honey bee, *sail on little bee, sail on,* he sings in

the fifties when you were so young that

bees meant bees, not love gone away we sing to get back.

You could step on one, get stung, cry to your mom till

the sting eased up, as Muddy's does when his love

buzzes home after having made *honey*

all around the world.

Or, in plain English, being unfaithful, like Muddy was.

He had an intelligent mien, songs you could trust,

cheeks gently sloped toward a mouth you can almost hear saying

go in peace, your sins are forgiven, amen.

Area E:

Between a rock and the place it's not—a shadow.

On Sundays we would drive out of town toward

Santiago Canyon and ritual emerged for control

—park the car, grab a kiss, grab the water, begin

our trek around a hill rising out of everything flat.

The desert sizzles with exposures you and I shun.

We climb agitation out of our bodies and minds,

carry our proud, serene selves to the very top,

feeling the place come and go, all the while

getting used to its power to lead to a spot where

openings stun: in the churning heart that turns

into an ear with no hands to block out

occasions of peace or the world in need roaring underneath.

Lingering (in Place)

My Mother was a Place

Gone nearly twenty years
she's still for me
a place.

I've been there
and let me tell you
it was dark, pearly dark
and warm.

In Latin, place is platea
or courtyard.

We were together there,
her skin extending to form
a being she could not yet see.

Outside, sipping tea,
she watched a monarch
land on a leafy fern then disappear.

Inside, coming to
slowly, I heard her cry now and then,
monarchs always on their way somewhere.

My birth disrupted the rhythm we had.
Now, when I want to restore its calm,
I find a courtyard, peer over the walls

and listen as she hums the Ave Maria,
surrounded by buds about to open,
surrounded by the grace of ripening fruit,
a monarch lingering in place on a fern.

Notes

In "Monarchs Fly Great Distances," the "Italian Argentine" who is quoted is Antonio Porchia. I used the following translation: Porchia, Antonio.Voices.Trans. W. S. Merwin. Port Townsend, WA: Copper Canyon Press, 2003.

Source of reference used in "The Cemetery Way": Nemec, Ludvik. The Great and Little One of Prague. Philadelphia: The Peter Reillyl Co., 1959.

The inspiration for the long poem,"Two Ways," arose when I participated in a silent retreat at the Shalom Spirituality Center in Dubuque, Iowa.Two or three times a day, I walked these paths, one on a paved walkway through Mt. Calvary Cemetery and the other on an unpaved walkway, a prairie grass restoration area on the grounds of the retreat center.

About the Author

Barbara Wuest, a graduate of UC-Irvine's MFA in Creative Writing, taught English and Creative Writing at Cardinal Stritch University in Milwaukee. Her poems have appeared in a variety of literary journals such as *The Cape Rock, Wind Literary Journal, Western Ohio Journal, Laurel Review, The Paris Review, Cincinnati Poetry Review, Dogwood, CrossCurrents, Oberon, The Beloit Poetry Journal, Wisconsin Academy Review* and others. She served as a poetry editor for the *Association of Franciscan Colleges and Universities (AFCU) Journal. Among Others*, a chapbook of poetry, was published by Finishing Line Press (2015). Her poetry collection, *Shadowy Third*, was published by Aldrich Press (2016). She also published a memoir, *Drive Gently* (2017). She and her husband Glen live in Milwaukee.

9 781947 465473